RAFAEL CASTEJON Y MARTINEZ DE ARIZALA

THE MOSQUE
OF
CORDOBA

Photographs:
ORONOZ

EDITORIAL EVEREST

Carretera León - Astorga, Km. 4,500 — Apartado 339 — LEON (España)

1.ª Reedición, 1973

I.S.B.N. 84-241-4713-8
Legal Deposit. LE.: 16-1973
© by EDITORIAL EVEREST-LEON
Printed in Spain - 1973

LITOGRAFIA EVEREST - Carretera León-Astorga. Km. 4,500 - LEON

THE ALJAMA MOSQUE OF CORDOBA

The Aljama Mosque of Cordoba, the great mosque of the Moslem West, is built on the shores of the Guadalquivir River, at the site previously occupied by the Latin-Byzantine Bassilica or Christian Cathedral of Saint Vincent, and before that by a great Roman temple and possibly before this by some delubrum, triumph or idolarium, of the natives or the Phenician or Greek settlers, since that was the location of one of the river ports of old Cordoba. Hence, for several thousands of years, Cordovans have been praying to divinities of very different creeds and religions at the same site.

This Mosque of Cordoba, for centuries the largest in the whole Islamic world, has an exceptional importance in the history of universal art, because it is the laboratory where new styles originate and for the first time very valuable stylistic elements appear, whose influence lasts many centuries and passes to other countries, both of the North of Africa and the European South.

Its genesis and general structure obey to the meeting of Eastern and Western traditions, vaguely reflecting the Christian bassilical influence, and it also reminds the Egyptian hypostyle temples and the Persian apadanes, inheriting the Greco-Roman classical tradition, dressed in Syrian and Mesopotamian galas and arriving at the merger of all of it in a new style called art of the Caliphate of Cordoba, Spanish-

1. *General view of the Mosque, with the large mass of the Cathedral in the center, seen from the Roman bridge over the Guadalquivir.*

2. *The Great Mosque, the fortress of Faith, in whose courtyard the fountains and orange blossoms recall the Believer's Paradise.*

3. *Southwestern angle of the Mosque with Alháquem II's portals.*

Mogreb architecture or art of the Moslem West.

Because the Mosque of Cordoba is the full consecration of the horse shoe arch, of such a pure Hispanic ascendancy, professor Gómez-Moreno has been able to say in all assurance that it is the Most Spanish monument in Spain, and he asserts that from the prehistoric cave of Menga until today, our country can not boast of any other building comparable to it in originality.

The Mosque of Cordoba, as Torres Balbás assures, inaugurates Spanish-Moslem art, comes to its zenith in the X century, with the extension made by Alháquem II, contemporaneous of the wonders of Medina Azahara, and spreads throughout the Peninsula with the reigns of Taifas, having as heirs the constructions of Almoravides and Almohades, and as farther removed descendants the Nazarite art of Granada, where the cycle of this art ends in the Peninsula. Somewhere else he has said

that in Cordoba, Rome comes to the end of the Caliphate.

In our time Chueca Goitia asserts that the Mosque of Cordoba is the last of the Hellenistic monuments made in the world.

HISTORICAL REMEMBRANCE

When at the beginning of the VIII century, in 711, the first formal contingents of Arabs or Chaldeans as they were then called landed in the Peninsula, the national territory was in the midst of a civil war, due to the eternal question of whether the monarchy should be inherited or elected.

Witiza had indicated his son Aquila II as the heir, but the Goth tradition of Warriors, magnates and bishops indicated Rodrigo, born in Cordoba, in the palace whose ruins are coming out these days, of his father Teudefredo, in turn son of king Chindasvinto, who, by his youth and ardor, stood out as a leader. Hardly designated he fought Aquila II, who had fled or taken

4. *The portal of St. Stephen, that the Arabs called the Visiers' Door, its archaeological filiation is well discussed.*

refuge on the North of the Peninsula, and in the temporary absence of the new king, the Witizan party calls the Arabs to help, and on the shores of the Guadalete they fight the battle in which Don Rodrigo dies, whose reign lasts less than a year. His followers have to flee, while the Witizans romain with their prerrogatives and properties under Arab dominion.

Cordoba had been rejuvenated at this time, by Egica and Witiza, as may be seen in the minting of contemporary coins. The Roman walls has been extended to the river line and a new cathedral, dedicated to St. Vincent, offered its three naves of a bassilical nature to the conquerors, who, having entered the city surely by a pact, respected one half of the temple to the Christians, and contented themselves with the other half, until 741.

This situation lasts almost half a century, the stage of the governors or emirs, dependent of Damascus, until the first Abderrahman arrives in Cordoba, who was the last offspring of the Omeya dynasty of the Orient, who after an almost novelesque flight reaches Spain and establishes a dynasty lasting more than two centuries. It is almost at the end of his long reign (755-788) in which, as he says in one of his poems, «I united with my sword the pieces of my kingdom, as a tailor unites with his needle the pieces of cloth to make a suit», that he decides on the construction of a new mosque, in addition to a new Alcazar or royal palace. Thus, he had prayed in half of the Christian temple, just as he had also lived in the old country palace of the Goth governors, called the «palace of Teodomiro», to which he gave the name of al-Rusafa, as a memento of the one his grandparents had near Damascus.

To erect this first Mosque, Abderrahman «the Immigrant», totally tears down the Christian temple, but he also almost totally used its elements, especially the columns of the bassilical naves. It seems that he starts the work in 785 and when he dies three years later (788) it is not fully com-

pleted, since his son Hixem I must erect the tower or minaret from where the muezzin calls to prayer. No indication of these data subsists, although Arab chroniclers are very precise in their indication; neither are there left any names of the builders who erected the same.

GENERAL DESCRIPTION OF THE MOSQUE

The Mosque of Cordoba is a rectangle 130 meters wide by 180 meters deep, with a surface therefore of 23.400 square meters.

It is inside a strong towered wall which gives it the aspect of a fortress —the fortress of faith—, and it consists of a large courtyard to the North, occupying almost one third of the total (es-sahn or Courtyard of the Orange Trees) and a roofed inside temple (chami).

The wall is crowned by embattlements of a staggering type, whose remote antecedent is in the Sassanid architecture of Persia, but which became such a part of all constructions in the Caliphate that by antonomasia they are called Cordovan embattlements.

The main door is on the North, called the Pardon door because on its porch sat the court of justice ofaan ecclesiatical nature that remitted tithes and fines to the delinquent, in the days in which the chapter had available large rents and extensive properties.

This door was largely modified in the XIV century, to this time belongs the splendid mudejar door covered with decorated plates, in whose centers alternate the words DEUS and AL-MULK LILAH (the empire and the power is only God's). It has very deteriorated paintings by Antonio del Castillo.

There is one other door on this northern front called the Caño Gordo (Thick Spring) door, through which it flows on its side, Greco-Roman in style of the XVII century, and beside it a popular altar-piece called of the Virgen de los Faroles (Our Lady

8

5. *Foreshortened view of a marvelous portal of Alháquem II, finely restored at the beginning of this century.*

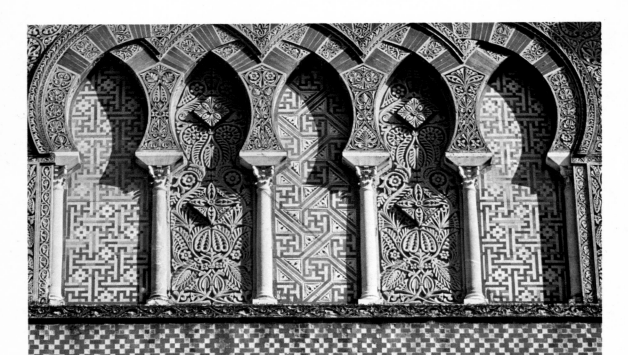

of the Lanterns), with a painting of the Assumption that burned down in 1928 and was substituted with another painted by the famous Romero de Torres.

Other doors leading to the courtyard are the Postigo de la Leche (the Milk Peepwindow) on the Western side, where in old times abandoned children were placed, of a decadent ogival style, with another analogous one on the Eastern side of a strong eccentricity, and further from the latter what is called the Puerta de los Deanes (the Deans Door), of moslem outline, although very reformed.

In the remainder of this Western face there are five doors giving access to the inside, to be described later, as well as on the Eastern side there are seven doors to the inside, apart from the one to enter the courtyard from that side, called of Sainte Catherine, plateresque, reformed in 1573, with leaves covered with bronze plates in the Caliphal style, and two coats of arms on the spandrels of its great arch representing the Arab minaret prior to its reform.

THE DOOR OF SAINT STEPHEN

This is the name given in modern times to the first great door between fortified towers, corresponding to the primitive mosque of Abderrahman I, through which the sovereign and his retinue entered, this being the reason for the dust-guard or embattlement cornice it has on the top. In its time it was called Bab-al-uzara or door of the visiers or ministers.

This door, the oldest in the Mosque, has been the object of educated archaeological arguments. Famous master Gómez-Moreno

6. *Detail of another Alháquem II portal with Cufic letterings in the center.*

7. *The today called St. Michael's peep-window, where the first passage-way with the Caliphal Castle gave, reformed in the XVIth century.*

8. *The Door named the Dove's Door, whose Arabian original was almost destroyed by the exquisite ogive decoration made toward the end of the XVth century.*

considered it as what remained of the previous Christian bassilica. Apparently the side decoration, very much corroded due to the poor quality of the stone, corresponds to mid IX century and the extension of the pre-caliph Abderrahman II, which confirms the Arabic inscription all along the intrados of the main arcade and ends on a horizontal band through the center of the tympanum, which corresponds to emir Mohamed I, son of the above, who completed this extension and indicates the date of 241 of the Hegira, 855 A.D.

Recently there have been found, while the inside subsoil was being removed, architectural remains of the homologous door which opened to the primitive Eastern door; these are preserved better and reproduce the same decoration of this door.

They are exposed on pilasters approximately where they were found. Arabian author Aben Adari says that this was then the firts time that work on stone was done in the Mosque.

This door of Saint Stephen has seen many reforms, possibly some during the Arabian epoch, such as the three blind small archs covering the main arch, this one being restored in the XIX century.

Along towards the South there is another door, with a poor Gothic decoration, called today the peep-window of Saint Michael, corresponding to an original passage way built by caliph Abdaláh between the Alcazar and the Mosque to enter the temple without having to mingle with the people, consisting of a great arch above the street under which the people passed by. This first passage way was destroyed a century later when Alháquem II made his extension and had built another passage way at the end of the street at the end of the Mosque.

It has already been said that in the time of these first emirs and caliphs, there was a great plaza next to the Mosque, occupied today by Saint Jacinto's Hospital, built in the XVI century with a beautiful Gothic door; the parades and military guards were performed there on the main door to the Alcazar, called by a Latin name, Bab Curia or Door of the Curia, because it gave access to the administrative offices or parts of the Caliphal palace.

THE PORTALS OF ALHAQUEM II

The three following portals, richly decorated, belong to the ostentatious extension made by Alháquem II. They have their correspondents in what was the Eastern façade of this extensión, mutilated and hidden by the extension made by Almanzor a short twenty years later. For this reason their remains, far from the inclemence of the weather, maintain their fine work and the simple coloring of the background, especially the one most to the South and at the end, commonly called the Puerta del Chocolate (Chocolate Door), because it had been inside a room where the canons used to meet for light repasts. This door has been the model for modern restorers in their outside work.

In effect the three portals leading out came to our time in a very poor condition due to the Westerly winds beating that façade, except the one in the center and its center arch, had been dubbed and a great part of its semi-destroyed decoration had been hidden.

Restoring their original composition has been a masterful job, carried out by architect Velázquez Bosco and the great Cordovan sculptor Mateo Inurria, so that the modern work by far surpasses the delicate old work. It is true that the restorer has used some license, such as carving some inscriptions to replace those swept by time, with a modern text in Arabic letters (aljamian) declaring that it was restored in the time of «sultan Alfonso son of Alfonso», that is, King Alfonso XIII, Faustino Rodríguez Sampedro being his minister.

All in all, the restoration has been a superb one, and has returned to universal art one of its greatest masterpieces.

The main arch has two blind windows on its sides, under an arch surmounted by another two bays with elegant serrated arch and marble lattices, all it adorned with a fine caliph style decoration, of Byzantine origin, done in stone and red brick mosaic tympani.

However, the most attractive thing of these portals is the small intercrossed archway surmounting the main arch, and the small, horseshoe shaped arches on crossing with each other already outline the domed ogive of such important consequences in the Gothic and mudejar styles.

That intercrossing of arcades, which is so characteristic of the art of the Caliphate

9. *Inside the temple there are remainders of old Arabian portals torn down for Almanzor's extension.*

10. *The simple Deans' Door is the access to the Orange Tree Courtyard. In the background a monument or Triumph to St. Raphael, Custodian Archangel of the City, erected in the XVIIIth century.*

of Cordoba, both in building and decoration, apparently has very remote and simple backgrounds in Mesopotamia, the present Irak; however, it has been in this monuments of the Andalusian Omeyas that it acquired full stylistic tones.

The center one of these three great portals underwent a large gothic reform in the XV century, when the Catholic Kings had their headquarters in Cordoba for the conquest of Granada, corresponding to the nave of the interior church. It is called the Puerta de la Paloma (the Dove Door), due to the representation of the Holy Ghost inserted in the Christian restoration. On the top it has a cornice with embattlement cresting of Arabian times, indicating its condition of a royal entrance.

In the angle a small door at a certain height is the old one to the passage way (sabbath) of the Arabs communicating with the Alcazar.

THE PORTALS OF THE EASTERN FRONT

If the portals of the Western sise have suffered the historical and hence artistic changes of the temple, those on Eastern side belong to only one moment, that of Almanzor's extension, towards the of our X century, the fourth of the moslem hegira.

Five of them have been totally restored, but the southernmost ones, two of them, continue offering a regretable and ruinous

14

11. *General view of the Eastern portals of Almanzor's time.*

state. The inscriptions on these façades are all religious, and the surahs or verses of the Koran copied in them have permitted remaking what remained of them, although others have been left blank, not knowing which they were.

The beauty of these five portals on this front can be compared to those of Alhá-quem II. There is in them an apparent return to a larger classicism within the caliphal style, as in the decorative side windows there appears the couple arch window, of such a strong hispanic tradition in the Spanish-Gothic and the Mozarabic art although the upper arcade does not have crossed arches, but some are an elegant and simple horseshoe, while others

are alternating with the serrated ones of the following portal. The whole is also of an extraordinary beauty.

We must indicate as restoration dates that the last scaffold was taken out in 1914, almost at the same time of the declaration of the First World War, and that the authors were the architect Velázquez Bosco and the sculptor Inurria.

The stoop on this front, increasing in height toward the South due to the slope of the ground, was paved with red sandstone tiles from Montoro.

The southern front of the Mosque, with many towers, does not have primitive doors or portals or decorations. The Christian centuries added some balconies toward the

15

12. *Details of a coupled arched window, not restored, on the Eastern side of the Mosque.*

southwest angle in the XV century, another stone balcony to the back of the Sacrarium, and a niche with the Virgen del Caminante, bordering the Puerta del Puente (the Bridge Door), (Bab Alcántara of the Arabs) in the XVII century. The miharab has a salient to the outside between two fortified towers but is withim its line, and Arabian authors say that it had in its middle a marble tablet with an allusive inscription, but it does not exist.

THE ORANGE TREE COURTYARD

The orange tree is a Persian name, and with the lime tree and other trees of the same family did not arrive in the West until approximately the XI century; there-fore, in the golden times of the Caliphate of Cordoba it did not exist in our country.

The name of Patio de los Naranjos (Orange Tree Courtyard), is Christian, and apparently the firts trees of this species were planted after the Reconquest, by Alfonso X el Sabio, (Alfonso X the Wise).

When Abderrahman III enlarges this courtyard he planted olive trees in it, and cypresses and laurel trees. The Arabs called it es-sahn, the equivalent of the Spanish word zaguán (entrance) or entrance court-yard.

Mosques courtyards, besides their prayer value the same as the inside, have fountains or ablution basins, where the believer puri-fies himself prior to praying. Possibly no original ones remain, except one on a Visigoth pilaster at the right of the inside entrance.

The present fountains are of mudejar tradition, and the large one, with four spouts, is completely baroque, as is a smaller one at the edge of the stoop.

For the moslems the mosque courtyards serve for varied public functions, besides the religious ones. On the north gallery there are usually students and alfaquíes (Islam priests), and above it there is usually the tower, for which reason they are called kotubas or kutubías, from the root káteb, student.

On the eastern gallery installed himself, sitting on a straw mat and assisted by two officers generally, the district judge, to whom petitioners went, with curious details which may be read in the anecdotic and unique «Historia de los jueces árabes de Córdoba», (History of the Arab judges of Cordoba), by Aljoxaní, of a wide publication in a Spanish edition.

The doctors or Ulemas delivered their lectures on the Western gallery. There taught the renowned Averroes, when the plebs, incited by the intransigent Almohade priests, pursued him and stoned him, and he had to flee, taking refuge in various places, until he arrived at Morocco, where he was benigningly welcomed and was the

16

advisor of the XII century sultan Yacub ben Yusuf.

Since the original VIII century courtyard was enlarged to the North in the X century and to the East at the end of the same by Almanzor, its general architecture has been slightly modified. This last part has a very large cistern for storing water.

Subsequent times of Christianity have added pilasters and crestings of a gothic style and have covered the entrance to the naves so as to have chapels in them.

THE TOWER

The word menara, from which comes alminar (minaret), and more rarely minaret, is applied by the Arabs to the second body or part of the tower, which if it were very large, as is that of this Mosque of Cordoba, received the name of as-sumua.

There existed a first one, corresponding to the primitive mosque, built by Hixem I, whose emplacement has been indicated in modern times with gray granite tiles, when the foundations were identified, about ten meters to the south of the present one (year 778).

When Abderrahman III enlarges the courtyard to the North, he builds a new minaret, who became the venerable grandfather of all the Arab towers of the moslem West, also marking its influence in all the Peninsula in future centuries, as happens with the mudejar towers in Aragon and Catalonia, and some of southern France and the square towers of the XIII and XIV centuries of northern Italy.

This Arabian tower lasts, as does an almond inside its shell, inside the present baroque tower. In the XVII century architect, Hernán Ruiz imprisons it with strong walls on its four sides and raises it to form drum bodies, some of which are very beautiful.

Of the Arabian aspect of the tower remain drawings and etchings permitting its ideal reconstruction. Inside itwas formed by two twin staircasis, which permitted going up one and down the other without meeting.

13. *The center street of the Orange Tree Courtyard, as seen from the staircase giving access to the temple through the Pardon Door.*

15. *Interior of the Western gallery of the Courtyard, where old pieces of the panelled ceiling are exhibited, where Islam's wise Ulemas taught, from where the great Averroes had to leave stoned by the populace.*

The present baroque appearance is gracious an is greatly praised by the historians of that style, such as Otto Schubert, who considers it the greatest monument of the times of Nora. The present tower is crowned by a Saint Raphael, by the sculptor Pedro de Paz, which was placed in the year 1664.

The Arabian tower was crowned with the classic stem with four golden balls inserted in a vertical axis ending in a silver color lily.

BLESSING ARCH AND ARABIAN TABLET

The door giving access inside the Mosque is called Arco de las Bendiciones (Blessing Arch), because in the days of the Reconquest the flags going to the war in Granada were blessed there. It is necessary to remember that since Cordoba (1236) and Seville (1248) were conquered, until Granada (1492) was conquered nearly two centuries elapse, during which the whole Cordovan region and the capital itself borders with the moors and is constantly under attacks and pillage.

Two arcades are appreciated in this Arco de Bendiciones, the outside one was built by Abderrahman III in the X century, and the inside one, more primitive, built by Abderrahman I at the end of the VIII century. The whole bay of the first one served to stop the collapse of the primitive one, which is seen at plain eye and is the whole façade bay.

Even more notable is the style difference of the capitals, of which the older are goth, with Byzantine cros with equal arms hewn by the Islamites, the second being caliphal in the style.

14. *Northern gallery of the Orange Tree Courtyard, with Christian reforms, as well as the beautiful tower of baroque appearance.*

16. *General view of the first Mosque built by Abderrahman I, with its varied collection of Roman and Byzantine capitals.*

17. *The Mosque's main nave, interrupted by the great construction of the Cathedral, and the Miharab in the background.*

Of this job, as well as of the enlargement of the courtyard to the North, there is an account on the beautiful tablet fixed to this wall, which in Cucic letters says in a Castillian translation:

In the name of Allah, the Clement, the Merciful/ the serf of Allah, Abderrahman, Prince of belie/vers, Annásir (Defender) of the Law of Allah, may Allah prolong his days | gave orders to build this façade and firm its foundations/for the honor of the ceremonies (of the cult) of Allah and preser/vation of his sacred prophecies which Allah permitted to be praised and remem/bered together with his name for which he expects/grattitude, great mercies and treasures together with/ permanent glory, prosperity and high renown. And this was completed/with the helps of Allah in the moon of Dulhichia/of the year three hundred forty six under the/direction of his freedman (rubbish) guazir and majordomo of his house (háchib)/Abdaláh ben Bedr. Made by Said ben Ayub.

Two Roman milestone columns have been placed at this portal, which were found when the foundations of the cathedral groin arch were built in the XVI century, and on the same façade there are others found in other Cordovan places.

The plateresque decoration of this portal was made in 1531 by bishop Fray Juan de Toledo.

A problem which has not yet been clarified is whether the nineteen portals of the naves opening to the courtyard had curtains, lattices, bronze plated doors or were totally open.

THE MOSQUE OF ABDERRAHMAN I

The Mosque of Cordoba was firstly a square 73 meters wide by 74 meters deep approximately, divided almost exactly through its half in a courtyard and chami or roofed temple.

Archaeologists argue on the background or antecedents of the Mosque of Cordoba, because the first eastern mosques were

22

18. *Columnar fust of the IXth century, typical sample of Byzantine art, a possible present from the Christian Emperor of Byzantium to Caliph Abderrahman II.*

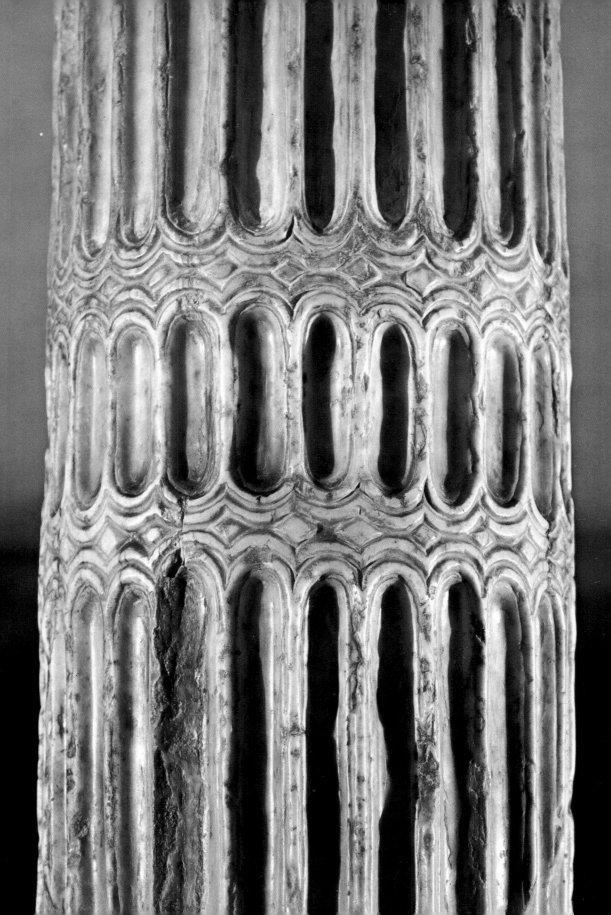

20. *The same colonnade seen diagonally, with Corinthian capitals with blue fusts and pink fust compounds.*

formed by a succession of naves parallel to the miharab, while this one of Cordoba confirms the construction of longitudinal naves.

A center nave, at the bottom of which was the orientation miharab, with five on each side, make the total of eleven which formed this first mosque. It has been discussed if they were four on each side, adding two at the end, when the first enlargement was made, but it is as doubtful as the archaeological and historical data on which the supposition is based.

These naves are formed by a series of colonnades, supported on elegant fusts of a columnar nature over which there are two series of arches, the lower horseshoe in shape, the upper one is a Roman arch. This arrangement, in which the lower arch works in the manner of a stay, is one of the greatest originalities of the Cordovan Mosque, giving it a special graciousness and lively elegance. In order to establish

the contrast, we must remember that many mosques are supported on stone or brick pillars, propping with heavy pieces of lumber which form a little agreeable grill.

The arches, in addition, are formed by yellowish stone wedgepieces, the frank calcareous stone of Cordoba, alternating with other red brick wedge-pieces, whose arrangement and bichromy, of goth background in Cordoba itself, continuing, as the horseshoe arch itself, a tradition which is prior to the Arab invasion, trascends fully not only in all the national territory, but goes beyond the borders, with a greater influence, logically, to the South in all of North Africa.

THE ENLARGEMENTS

As Cordoba grew, as the capital of the Spanish Arabian empire, the successive emirs and caliphs enlarged the Mosque, as Abderrahman II in 848, Abderrahman III (only the courtyard and the tower) in 951, Alháquem II in 961-970, and finally Almanzor in 987.

The first enlargements were made in a

19. *Partial aspect of Alháquem II's extension, with a beautiful colonnade of pink fusts from Cabra alterbating with blue marble from Cordoba.*

25

21. *The space behind the choir of the Cathedral was beautifully decorated in the first half of the XVIth century, building three chapels with alabaster reliefs of Italian manufacture.*

longitudinal sense, always with the same width, but the last one by Almanzor is done on the eastern side, in almost forty per cent of the total. The group is almost a square occupying 23.400 meters of surface.

The two first parts of the Mosque are made with materials from previous buildings and the two second parts with materials expressly carved for it.

It is known that the colonnades of the first part come mostly from a previous Christian temple, especially the center nave, with beautiful fusts of rose color marbre from Cabra. On the ten side naves, five on each side, alternating columns of the same marble and columns of gray granite, of unknown origin, since that stone comes from the northern part of the province, the Pedroches Valley.

In the enlargement made by Abderrahman II, which adds eight arcades to the previous twelve, there are columns of a very varied nature; many of gray marbles, expressly brought when the Roman theater of Merida was destroyed, where Abderrahman II built the great alcazaba (called by him hisn or fortress), defending the great bridge over the Guadiana river. Tradition remembers that this emir owned a tamed African elephant which brought many columns on tow, and when the animal died he had hung one of its tusks from the ceiling (which still exists) and placed a tablet on the wall relating this service. This tablet has disappeared.

In the enlargement made by Alháquem II, consisting of twelve new arcades, the colums expressly cut from a quarry, alternate between those made of blue marble from Cordoba and those made of red marble from Cabra, making a very nice effect. Seen diagonally they are all of the same color.

Almanzor's enlargement also offers columns of the same blue marble, alternating with others of a grayish color, both coming from the Cambrian calcareous stone of the Cordovan range, but its fusts lack the robust elegance of the previous ones. Let us remember that Almanzor in person worked in this enlargement to the mosque in an attempt to flatter divinity and redeem his sins. Also to be remembered is the anecdote of an old woman whose house was located inside the impressment ordered by Almanzor for enlarging the Mosque and who did not retract in her pretension of keeping the house of her parents and the palm tree on the courtyard, in the shadow of which the house rested, until the great ruler, besides compensating her very well, had a house built for her on a place selected by her, exactly the same as the old one, and moved the loved palm tree to the new courtyard.

Some columns bear the name of the quarryman who cut them, and in the Christian centuries Christs and virgins were

22. *Side of the domer or access room to Alháquem II's extension, with noble intercrossings of arcades.*

26

24. *The Mosque's main nave in the section corresponding to the notable extension made by Alháquem al Mustansir biláh.*

grossly carved on them which originate pious popular legends. Both Arabs and Christians have always thought they see faces and writings on the natural veins of the stone.

THE SKYLIGHTS

A tale of «The Thousand and One Nights» says that somewhere in the West there is a beautiful mosque on whose center nave open three alcoves or domes through whose windows divine light pours over the believers. This is the Cordovan mosque.

The first skylight dome was above the three end arcades of the first construction by Abderrahman I, in front of his miharab.

Today it is replaced by the magnificent Arabian panelled ceiling which has been rebuilt in all that center nave. A beautiful horseshoe arch, today re-covered with gothic adornments, the first to cut the nave crosswise, supported it on the northern side, the same that gave access to the possible first macsura or reserved enclosure for the caliph and his retinue.

The second skylight opens the enlargement made by Alháquem II, giving it an ingress one of the most splendid serrated arches of the temple and supported on interlaced arcades, each one of which is a real jewel of universal architecture. The Western side disappeared at the time of the Catholic Kings when the first nave of the church-cathedral was

23. *The most beautiful interlaced arcade in the Mosque, it gave access to the Macsura, reserved for the Caliph and his court.*

erected, and the Eastern side is shut up on its lower part to form a sort of crypt which served as a royal mausoleum since the XIV century, where the Kings of Castille Ferdinand IV and his son Alfonso XI were buried; their graves are today in the Real Colegiata de San Hipólito, founded for this purpose. This enclosure is covered by a dome above crossed arches, to be mentioned later, and the whole has the name of Villaviciosa Chapel, because for centuries there was in it the great altar of the cathedral nave on its side, where the Virgin of that appellation had been, and is today in the main altar of the second cathedral. When this enclosure was restored at the end of the XIX century, a restoration of the paintings which re-covered the crossed arcade of the vault was started, to be rubbed off later unpremeditatedly due to archaeological arguments.

The third skylight is in the vestibule of the third and present miharab. It also has groin arches on the walls and ceiling, and is covered by an admirable sod made dome. The whole, re-covered with Byzantine mosaic, a special present of Emperor Constantino Porfirogénito, is one of the marvels of worl art. Since the word mosaic is strange to the Arabs, they called this material musafah, foseifas and similar words. Its southern side or alkibla is formed by the unique façade of the miharab, which reflects the many colored lights of the mosaic and numberless inscriptions, which make a unique gem out of it.

THE VAULTS OVER ARCHES

The most original architecture of the Mosque of Cordoba is probably in the vaults covering these skylights in the main nave and some of the side naves, which were called «al-cobba» in Arabic, or dome, from where comes the Spanish word «alcoba» or bed chamber.

These Arab domes are built by erecting stone arcades on the walls, which intercross

with the various geometrical combinations, leaving small lacunar spaces, filled with masonry, but decorated in the form of small domes or shells, all unequal in the tracing and decoration, both the formal or constructive ones and decoration small domes.

The origin of these vaults is not known to this day, since those found in some country un the Orient are of a later date. What makes their import more probable is that here they are in full evolution development, without the hesitations of all new things. The hypotheses divide between a far Iranian origin, not verified, and a local tradition whose connection is lost.

The unquestionable fact is that these first vaults over arches which appear in full splendor in the Cordovan Mosque, as so many elements of culture, pass to the European countries, and through the Mozarabic art and the Jacobean route spread toward the north, giving a century later beautiful examples in the Mozarabic and ogive art, later inherited in the gothic art of central Europe, where the classical ribs of ogival art are now only decorative arcades, following the route of all elements that having been constructive end being a decoration, in a far inheritance of their forbears.

Today, only four caliphal vaults over arches exist in the Mosque of Cordoba, three in front or the miharab and one in the axis itself of the main nave. But it is sure that this last one had its side ones such as those preceding the miharab, both because in all mosques of this type, of the X century, the head was similar to the feet of the building, and Alháquem II, the caliph who built it and his builders used this principle, and because there are old descriptive writings on the Mosque-Cathedral, mentioning these three domes or cupolas, seen by their authors. The one on the western side was destroyed at the end of the XV century, in the days of the Catholic Kings, when a first nave of a cathedral was built inside the Mosque; and that on the eastern side

25. *Kibla was the name the Arabs gave to the wall in the back of the Mosque, where the miharab opens.*

probably subsists disfigured by the exuberant mudejar decoration of the Royal Chapel built by Henry II in the XIV century.

Therefore, in the General History of Art, the Mosque of Cordoba, almost intact in our time, is a rich vein furnishing first hand elements to learn of stylistic evolutions and once more confirms the role of our Peninsula as a transmitter of culture.

THE KIBLA

The kibla, or southern part, is, by antonomasia in mosques the southern wall where the miharab opens.

Here in Cordoba, the kibla wall has three portals which are richly decorated with Byzantine mosaic, the center one of the miharab, and two smaller side ones: the one on the left gives access to the sabbath or passage way through which the Caliph came to the temple from his castle, and the one on the right, which goes into a room where the sextons kept lamps and other objects of the cult. Today it is very transformed into a baroque chapel and serves as a Capitulary Hall.

This last portal is totally modern, made in Spanish shops early in the century copying its analogous one, because when the great painting of The Supper, by Céspedes, which gave the name to this chapel or enclosure was removed from the place it occupies, there was nothing behind it, that is, it had been destroyed. As regards the one giving access to the sabbath, it also has its lower parts restored, even the hole though which the mimbar or pulpit was put away.

This wall of the kibla supports the three great cobbas or cupolas forming a vestibule for the miharab, and its set of arcades sustains them with unique elegance.

The center one, of a marvelous mosaic decorative richness, resolves the architectural problems with linked arcades over columellas and pendentives, leaving holes for marble lattices and being covered with the small center echinus. A cornice of a whitish edge bordering that cupola, is not mosaic, but each piece of its octagonal side is a superb ceramics piece with golden or metallic reflection decoration, whose presence in this X century building has discovered a very previous origin for the XIV century works in Malaga and Granada.

From the center of the cupola with echinus hangs a golden chain, which in its time sustained a great silver lamp or atanor, with one thousand glass cups for oil burners, as well as another two on the side ones.

We point out the two great panels decorated on marble, which on each side form the door-jambs of the great arch of the miharab, whose work represents an oriental motif of a millenary tradition, the hom or tree of life, formed by a trunk producing interlaced branches with foliage and symbolical fruits, and even animals toward the last part of caliphal art, because this model is stylistically repeated in Medina Azahara and great palatial buildings of the time.

The arcades and cupolas of these domes notre-covered with mosaic were once painted, with colors and drawings in tone with it, and a close visual examination still discovers what remains.

THE MIHARAB

The miharab or niche of orientation is an essential part of all mosques, which indicates the believer the direction of Mecca, toward which he must direct his prayers. In many mosques in the Islamic world the miharab is a niche or closet on the wall, but in the Mosque of Cordoba it is a small room recalling Christian chapels, whose influence is argued.

Since those who ordered the construction of the Cordovan Mosque were of Syrian origin, it was oriented to the South, as others in the West, although later (the mosque of Medina Azahara itself, built in 940) they are correctly oriented to the Southeast.

Chroniclers relate that on the same day that

26. *Pillar of the vestibule of the miharab with arcade haunches.*

the great Caliph Abderrahman III died, his heir and successor held a meeting of the Council of visiers or ministers to take two fundamental agreements, the protocol of moving the corpse to the rauda or royal cementery in the Alcazar of Cordoba, and the enlargement of the Mosque, proposing in the latter case the demolition of the old parts, due to the incorrect orientation, or the enlargement in the previous direction. The case well discussed and was decided by the great judge of Cordoba Mohamed el Balutí, who «had his beard wet with tears» and ordered the previous orientation, since Allah had listened to his ancestors' prayers filling them with favors and largesse. It is also said that due to this incorrect orientation for moslem liturgy the intransigent Almohades, in the XII century, did not wish to pray in the Mosque of Cordoba and established the capital of Andalus in Seville. Due to the absidal structure, both the miharab of the first mosque and the two successive ones, had a salient outside, the two first ones recognizable in the pertinent archaeological excavations.

Chroniclers relate how in building the last and present one, the pair of columns and capitals supporting the main arch of the miharab had been disassembled from the previous one, and in effect they are typical examples of the IX century. The white alabaster columns, with beautiful channelings flanking that second miharab, seem to come from Byzantium itself, as a present from those emperors.

The great arch of the present miharab is totally re-covered of Byzantine mosaic. Since the Middle Ages it was covered by a wooden retable with valuable boards, but when it was removed, at the end of the XVIII century, it was found that the lower parts were destroyed almost to a height of one meter, and the Chapter entrusted its restoration to the violinist Pompeyo, very capable in craftmanship, who made the reform with baroque drawings and pieces

27. *Side cupola in the vestibule of the miharab, with interlaced arcade.*

29.   *Upper front of the miharab's façade, in which inscriptions and mosaics harmonize in delightful combinations.*

of glass, which give contrary light reflections, even if the whole is nice to the eyes.

The two pairs of columellas supporting the great arch, come likewise from the IX century miharab, two are bluish and the other two are a very brecious red marble (apple like, it was called by Arabian chroniclers). The capitals are typical models of the indicated century.

THE GREAT CUFIC TABLETS

This Cordovan Mosque keeps almost all the inscriptions fixed in the Arabian epoch. The most beautiful is the one in the Villaviciosa Chapel, written in elegant Cufic characters (whose name derives from Kufa, the City in Persia), as corresponds to every text of the Islamic religion. This tablet, originally fixed on the wall of the kibla, was taken out in the XVII century to carve on its back the funeral lauds to a canon; but in the year 1897, with the initiation of the

modern restorations, it was re-discovered when the pavement was removed. The translation of this beautiful tablet is the following:

In the name of Allah, the Merciful, the Clement. He confesses to Allah that truly there is bo other God but Him. The angels and those who invoke eternal knowledge and justice, also repeat, there is no other God but Him, the Omnipotent, the Wise. What Allah decrees is complied with. There is no strength and power but in Allah. The blessing of Allah on Mohammed, last of the Prophets and Prince of those sent. May he be reverenced in the Universe. The Imam, serf of Allah, Alháquem al Mustansir biláh, Prince of velievers, successor in his faith, his vicar among his serfs, keeper of his precepts, defender of his prohibitions and grateful for his benefits, ordered this enlargement, which was completed with the

30.   *The great miharab arch, with marvelous decoration in polychromed mosaic, framed by elegant Cufic letterings.*   ▶

28.   *The magnificent cupola in the center of the kibla, embellished with Byzantine mosaics, one of the gems of all universal art.*

37

31. *A pair of IXth century columns propping the miharab's arch.*

help of Allah and as he ordered, under the direction of his freedman and háchib Cháfar ben Abderrahman, may Allah please him, with the aspect of a fortress and the complement of its arcades in the year three hundred fifty eight (971 A. D.). Praised be Allah Lord of the Universe.

The beautiful letters with which this tablet is engraved, make it an epigraphical document of the first order, used today in Moslem universities.

Other tablets fixed in this place have a secondary interest, one is visigoth, others are gothic, and two are Arabian, brought from the territory of Granada, which are funeral tablets for Moorish chieftains.

THE INSCRIPTIONS ON THE MIHARAB

The Mosque of Cordoba has a great number of inscriptions, some have disap-

peared, but sufficient subsist, which have a religious value, and above a historical value, to make them more valuable. The proliferation of names of caliphs, ministers and important people bring suspicions of lack of religiousness in this liberality of names to the Islamics, who wish that only the name of Allah appear in the temple.

The front of the miharab is rich in writings formed with the Byzantine mosaic itself. Over the great arch there is a writing in deep blue signs on a golden background, indicating the first of the one hundred names of Allah. Its translation is:

In the name of Allah, the Clement, the Merciful, outside of whom there is no other God, the King, the Saint, the Saviour, the Faithful, the Custodian, the Strong, the Powerful, the Lofty, blessed Allah, far from Him the gods associating him.

32. *Magnificent decorative panel, engraved in marble, forming a door-jamb in the miharab.*

The great golden writing on cobalt blue background, that serves as a frame for the great arch of the miharab in two parallel lines although mutilated in its lower parts, has the following translation from the original:

...Allah knows the hidden and manifest things. He is the powerful, the full of piety. He is the living one. There is no other God but Him. Invoke him by offering him a pure cult, Praised be Allah, Lord of the Universe. Blessed be the Imam al Mustansir biláh, serf of Allah, Alháquem,

33. *Great conch, one piece, covering the interior of the miharab.*

34. *Octagonal interior in the miharab, where the Sacred Koram was deposited; in this room only the Imam, as supreme priest of Islam, could go in.*

Prince of Believers, may Allah give him prosperity = for the work of this holy temple which exceeds all other memorable construction in the comfortable amplitude.... = ... what is over them and over it in decorations and its construction was completed by his virtue and order. May the blessing of Allah come over Mohammed. Health = The Imam al Mustansir biláh serf of Allah, Prince of believers, may Allah praise him, ordered his freedman and háchib Cháfar ben Abderrahman, may Allah have pity of him, to take care of the construction of this temple, completed with the help of Allah = under the inspection of Mohamed ben Támlih, Ahmed ben Nassar, Jayd ben Háxim, of the Prefect's guard and of Motárrif...

Finally, in golden letters on a red background, there is an inscription in the imposts of the same great arch, that begins at the right of the looker and ends on the left, whose translation is:

In the name of Allah the Merciful, the Clement, praise to Allah who led us to this place as we could not be led if Allah did not lead us. The delegate of our Lord was sent with the truth for this purpose. The Imam al Mustansir biláh, serf of Akkah, Alháquem, Prince of believers = may Allah favour him, ordered his freedman and háchib Cháfar ben Abderrahman, may Allah please him, to add these two supports to what was built with the holy fright of Allah and his help. It was completed in the moon of dulhicha of the year four and fifty two hundreds (354 H., 964 C).

Inside the miharab there are other inscriptions, as well as in all the inside cobba, at the foot of the columellas and in the most diverse places, which are praises to Allah, remembrance of the preces, and signatures of the authors of the decoration, but all of them coincide in the sense of the above, as suitable for the place on which they are located.

THE CAPITALS OF THE MOSQUE

In the monotonous severity of the Mosque, the series of capitals, considered as a whole, constitutes a real archaeological museum.

In its first parts there are pure Roman capitals, of the most beautiful outline, and then the whole range of late Roman or Paleo-Christian which perdure and lengthen the classical module, with rather European influences, recalling the Merovingian and Carolingian times, poorly known in France, and with a difficult classification.

The Byzantine alternate with them, some of classical purity in that style, which may be recognized for their prismatic shape and palmer decoration, an medleys of both; one can not forget that in this first epoch almost all are carried there, or come from

43

other buildings, although mostly from the previous Christian bassilica.

In the enlargement made by Abderrahman II, in the second half of the IX century, there are also pure Roman and post Roman capitals, having in mind that during this reing the classical capitals were copied rigorously. But an eastern current enters at this time, more Mesopotamic than Syrian, Bagdad has beaten Damascus, current seen in decorations in the shape of a basket, channeled abacus and other signs described by master Gómez-Moreno, who indicates eleven capitals expressly carved, among them the four on the arch of the great miharab, which serve as a model.

In the splendid enlargement carried out by Alháquen II, all capitals of a classical tradition, have scarce decoration, perhaps due to the austerity of the religious building, as one must have in mind that this Caliph and the great school of contemporaneous builders and decorators have just built the great palatial city of Medina Azahara, and did not stop from reforming it constantly. In these capitals there is no more variance than the Corinthian over the blue columns and the compound ones over the red ones. Some have light red paint lines on their stalks.

Almanzor's enlargement also offer, as construction of original elements, capitals similar to the above, with no decoration, all equal, except that, contrary to the previous one, the compound are on blue fusts and the simple Corinthians over reddish gray columns. It may be assured that when these alternatives are not present, the columns have been removed in subsequent times.

It is certain that in the columns of the Cordovan Mosque is where the evolution of the capital may be followed at its best, from the pure Roman types to the classical caliphal shapes.

35. *Entrance arch to the sabbath, communicating with the Caliph's castle.*

44

THE PANELLED CEILINGS

The whole Mosque, from the stylistic point of view, is a summary of the High Middle Ages, whose original elements are recognized both in Europe and in the Orient, and located generally in our Peninsula in the period called Latin-Byzantine, to change slowly into the Arab-Byzantine.

The exception to this is the general roofing of the temple, the panelled ceilings of a noted Syrian origin which now come to Spain and originate the great hispanic school of white carpentry.

But these plain roofings, with large panels, carved and painted, over enormous beams which are also decorated, may be said to be the only element which is frankly foreign in the Cordovan Mosque, although it is soon a second nature and reaches the classicism in our country.

The decoration of these panels and beams consists of ample and simple geometrical loops, with scarce vegetable themes bordered by the stripe of rosettes which is so typical of the Byzantine. The backgrounds are painted red, blue and green, with yellows and some golden above all in the rosettes. The overall effect, with the loops and polychromy, is delightful.

All along the nave and crosswise to the beams, there was a narrow panel or dado, also decorated and with Alcoranic versicles, closing the ceiling with a panel, which has not been placed in the modern restoration, which shows the beam heads bare, short of this detail. All of the panelled ceiling known today seems to be the work of Alháquem II.

Early in the XVIII century and under the excuse of ruin, these panelled ceilings were removed and substituted by baroque vaults made of raddle and gypsum, of which a large part subsists. Modern restorations have again placed many original panels, which had been abandoned or used

36. *Detail of the arch of the sabbath, next to which was the door for keeping the mimbar or preaching pulpit.*

as angle rafters on the roof. More than seventy diverse decorative drawings have been recognized to date. Some have been placed museum— style in the galleries of the Orange Tree Courtyard. The panels which were seriously damaged have been copied faithfully and repainted with original colors by famous present painters.

THE LIGHTING OF THE MOSQUE

The natural lighting of the Mosque was sufficiently ensured by the great arcades giving access from the courtyard, and the large windows with lattices at the end of the naves oriented to the South. In addition, the small lattices on the side walls gave an inclined light of a great beauty, seen today in the part enlarged by Alháquem II, since the construction of Christian chapels closed most of those windows and it was necessary to open skylights on the roofs, above all when the baroque vaults were built early in the XVIII century.

The artificial lighting, much praised by Arabian authors and described in detail, has an Islamic liturgical precision, especially during the whole month of the Ramadan. Allah is the light of heaven and earth, says a sura of the Koran, and all Moslem peoples take pains to provide the mosques with lamps; they fill the temples with luxurious chandeliers of an official nature or with humble lamps brought by the faithful believer; they are very necessary for the last prayer in the evening and many times for the first one in the morning.

There were hundreds of lamps in the whole temple; their number is different in accordance with the times, some people cite 113, others 280, and Macari indicates that only made out of latten or gilt brass there were 224, all having glass vases for oil burners; not a single one of them has remained.

There are many descriptions of the three silver lamps (turaia) located in the three cobbas of the ante-miharab, especially the

37. *The beautiful tablet, in Cufic characters, explaining the extension made by Alháquem II.*

38. *Prototypes of capital existing in the Mosque: Roman (1); Byzantine (2); and Caliphal (3 and 4) with no ornaments; Above the latter, on a modillion, the Islamic profession of Faith: «There is no God but Allah, and Mohammed is his Prophet».*

1

2

3

4

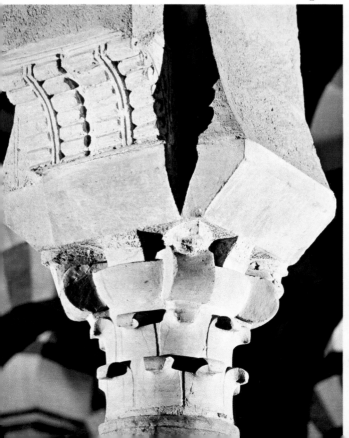

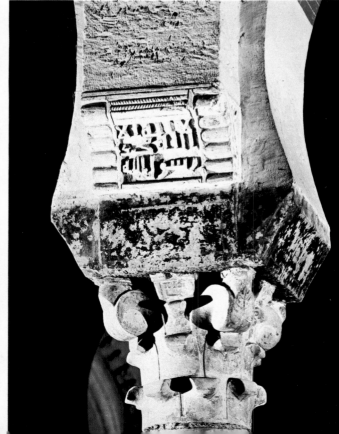

40. *The beautiful panelled ceiling, Syrian in tradition, with nearly eighty models of artistic tracing.*

center one (at-tannur), which bore more than one thousand oil lamps; between the three of them there were more than one thousand four hundred...

The oil consumption is accurately indicated by many authors, 24 pounds each night and lamp, seven quarters during the Ramadan and other various data. When Almanzor had the bells from the cathedral of Santiago de Compostela brought, he had them hanging upside down and full of oil and lamps.

Nine large green wax tapers burned on Fridays in front of the miharab.

Modern authors (Amador de los Ríos, Girault de Prangey, Torres Balbás) also poner the marvelous effect of the lights on the gilting of the panelled ceilings and more so on the polychromy of Byzantine mosaics, which would make the forms more aereal and subtle, as has been widely noted with the installation of indirect lighting in 1970, which has made the ceilings a truly fantastic thing.

THE PAVEMENT OF THE MOSQUE

Almost through our time it has been an archaeological problem trying to find the way the Mosque was originally paved. It has reached our time brick tiled and with cooked clay tiles.

When at the end of the XIX century the official era of restorations started, paving was started with large white marble tiles, removing lauds and funeral tablets that the Christian centuries had spread with profusion in the temple. Many of them have been placed in the gothic nave of the first Major Chapel, although the majority were already there.

Some Arabian chronicler emphatically talks of the reflection of the light on the miharab floor, which seemed to be made of silver, which makes one suppose that the place was paved with white marble; of course, there is some inside and perhaps there was some in front also, in the macsura

or enclosure reserved for the Caliph and his court.

The inside pavement has all around it a sufarce groove in the manner of a wide furrow, it is a popular belief that is was made by pilgrims going through there walking in a kneeling position. Nothing is farther from the truth, since in that place only entered the Imam or religious chief, who usually was the Caliph himself or a high category substitute, such as the Judge of Judges (cadí al-codáa) or a similar one. The truth is that that furrow or groove responds to the liturgical precept of foreseeing the fall to the floor of the sacred book, the Koran, which always had to be at a level higher than the Imam's feet, impure despite his category.

The total of the Mosque was earthen, as in man other mosques in the Islamic world, since the ritual prayer of a good Moslem requires that the forehead touch the earth, the same as the palm of the hand through the elbow, and sitting on the ground. It is clear that on the ground they spread rugs fine carpets, straw mats and even individual mats (lebda) which many believers carry under their armas when they attend the five ritual prayers in the day.

One of the services the Mosque had was stamping and sprinkling the earthen floor in order that no dust may rise. In the Cordovan archives there are deeds that every four years were executed by the corporation of the city, already in Christian times, paying for this service with the fruit of the orange trees in the courtyard, since during festivities and processions there was a great amount of dust that damaged clothing and cult objects.

To solve this difficulty, the corporation of the city during the Renaissance centuries compelled the founders of chapels and burial grounds to pave at their cost the nave in front of their place, and in this

41. *The great altar of the Royal Chapel decorated by Enrique II de Trastamara, during the second half of the XIVth century.*

42. *Dome of the Royal Chapel, over whose Arabian ornament mudejar decoration was made in the XIVth century.*

43. *Southern arch of the Royal Chapel with mudejar decoration of the XIVth century.*

44. *Beautiful Gothic tablet of the XVth century, signed by Pedro de Córdoba, surely the painting that is the best in the Cordovan Mosque.*

manner it was possible to tile the large temple.

The three oldest parts of the temple have been tiled with white marble slabs in modern times, Almanzor's enlargement remaining with bricks, indeed with level differences already equalled by Caliph Abderrahman III, but which the modern restorations have again unlevelled unnecessarily.

COMMUNICATION WITH THE ALCAZAR OF THE CALIPHS

Since the great Aljama Mosque and the Alcazar where the Caliphs resided, surely

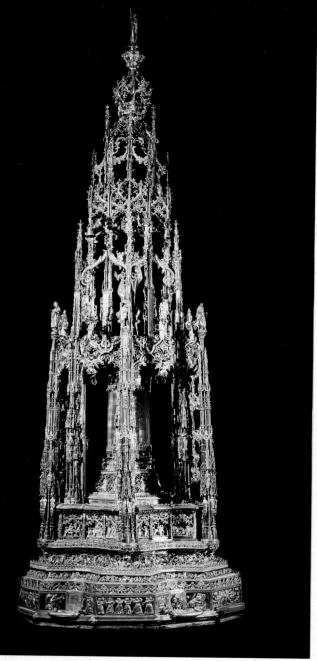

45. *The unique Gothic Custody made in the XVIth century, twins sister of the one in Toledo, both done by the German goldsmith Enrique de Arfe.*

an old Visigoth Hall and perhaps a great Roman palace before that, have bordering façades, although at a divergent angle to the South, the access of the sovereign and his court to the major temple, where, at the least on Fridays, and as the Imam or higher priest of the Islamic religion he had to lead the prayer, was easy.

But in the days of Emir Abdalah, grandfather of the great Abderrahaman III, there was built between both buildings a covered passage way, under a stone vault formed by a great arch over the street, whose archaeological traces and sturdy foundations exist today. We already mentioned this passageway or sabbath when we described the peep-window of Saint Michael, made at the end of the IX century.

When the Mosque is extended by Caliph Alháquem II approximately one century later, that first passage way is torn down and another one built, joining the two southern angles bordering Mosque and Alcazar, formed by a true gallery on columns, similar to an inside nave, and glass windows through which the people saw the sovereign and his retinue go by.

On Fridays and days of religious festivities, the people knelt with great praises and religious phrases, while the servants threw baskets of dirhemes, the silver coin equivalent to our peseta or franc of normal times.

This corridor lasted until the year 1610, in which due to its state of ruin it was ordered destroyed by Bishop Fray Diego de Mardones. Christian people called it «los arquillos» (small arches) and under them many episodes developed through the centuries regarding local history, such as the oath of the Campo de la Verdad (Field of Truth), taken by Cordovan Leader Alfonso de Montemayor when he defended the city from the allied armies of the sultan of Granada and Don Pedro el Cruel (1368).

A curious note is the melancholy anecdote of the last Caliph of Cordoba, a Hixem III who reigned for three years amid rebellions and revolutionary convulsions, who on being deposed and exiled, his life spared due to his personal kindness, spent the last night with his wives and children, in this passage way, gloomy and cold inside the temple, and asked the soldiers guarding him a piece of bread for the children and blankets

46. *The majestic Cathedral nave built inside the Mosque, began in the XVIth century, containing beautiful works of art, such as the Palomino retable, and the choir by Duque Cornejo.*

47. *«La Cena» (The Supper) by Cordovan prebendary Pablo de Céspedes, student with Michelangelo, who brought the origins of the Renaissance to Spain.*

to cover themselves. That was the sad end of a dynasty which had given Cordoba days of glory and power full of splendor.

THE STRAIN OF THE MOSQUE

With elements which are traditional some of them, and others of new contribution, the Cordovan Mosque forges an original style, with a great Byzantine cognation, thus starting the Hispanic-Moslem art or Caliphal art, which dies seven centuries later in the exquisite sweet-ness from Granada of the Nazarite art.

But it even jumps over the Renaissance, and both because of the survival of Moorish artists and the infiltration of Islamic themes in the Spanish soul, the Christian reigns of the Low Middle Ages continue to have in temples, palaces and craftmanships, the assemblies and motifs forged in the Islamic epoch, producing the mudejar style, so purely Spanish, that impregnates, almost up to our time, our vernacular arts. One may study and follow those influences in the great specialists works, of which our soil has magnificent examples.

Outside our territory, along the Arabian countries on the shores of the Mediterranean, up to those which are frankly oriental, there is also an influence, which in the closest ones, such as Morocco and Algeria, have arrived in all the Granadine purity until early in this century, as a national art, prior to getting modern currents.

Many craftmanships in ceramics, metals, Cordovan leathers and embossed leathers, jewels and textiles and all that the popular soul is able to produce, including clothing and customs, dances and songs, have inherited the unique stamp of that Hispanic-Arabian civilization which for the common man, due to the influence of the last foreign invasions of Almoravides and almohades coming from Morocco, are called in our country the work of Moors.

As regards the far influence, through the art of the Mozarabics, in medieval European styles, such as the Romanic and the Gothic, the inheritance of many themes is very patent, and in many cases it forms combinations between both stylistic influences, making them more beautiful and harmonic.

RELIGIOUS LIFE IN THE MOSQUE

In addition to the five ritual prayers that a good Moslem must say along the day, the mosques served as a great meeting place or public assembly hall, which really is the etimology of «aljama». It has been mentioned that from the mimbars or pulpits the decrees or legal provisions were enacted, the people was communicated of great events, flags and armies were blessed when they left for the battleground, and were gloriously received upon their return from the gazúas, generally loaded with booty and prisoners. The judges usually sit in the courtyards, and also teachings, both elementary and higher are given there.

The Imam or religious head of Islam (salvation) is the Caliph, who directs the prayer on Friday, the sacred day for Mos-lems, although he may delegate in the mocri (preacher) or the judge (cadí al-codáa) or great cadi of Cordoba.

Preaching is made from the mimbar, a large pulpit with seven stairs in front, of which really marvelous copies were made in Cordoba, some of which are kept in Morocco. The one in Cordoba disappeared a long time after the Reconquest. It was located on the left side of the miharab, with nine large green wax tapers in front, during religious festivities, and outside of them, it was hidden in the room of immediate access to the sabbath. Atop wooden platforms raised lightly they repeated recitals and prayers, due to the large size of the temple.

The Koran, sacred book of the Islamic religion, written by the prophet Mohammed, in Cufic characters, was placed on an easel, which also served as box or chest (dikké) its detailed description, the wood with encrusted precious stones, is very detailed by Arab historians, and very venerated, because it had four pages stained with the blood of Caliph Otmán, one of the Prophet's Companions. This copy was taken by the Almohades and their political successors, the benimerines, who carried as an amulet in their war expeditions the said book, and lost in a ship that was lost in the Straits of Gibraltar.

Mosques have their own properties or assets (habús, plural habices), and the Cordovan aljama came to have large amounts, with which care was taken of, besides the needs of a material nature of the temple, tapers and oils, the many employees and servants, the ritual alms and even the house for poor pilgrims (dar-el-sadaka or alms house), which bordered the Mosque on its western side, at the side of which was the mansion of the judges and consequently in the last times it was known as the house of the Beni Rushd, the family of the Averroes.

Special mention is deserved by the muezzins who call to prayer from the roofs of the mosques, who where well paid due to their beautiful voices, the Andalusians were to have a great fame due to the melodic

48. *The Inca's Chapel, in the Cordovan Cathedral, is one of the most solid linsk of Spanish-American culture.*

inflections they gave their chants, to whom tradition assigns the origin of the saetas or pious songs.

THE NAVES OF THE CATHEDRAL

On the 29th of June of 1236, Saint Peter's and Saint Paul's day, the king of Castille Ferdinand III the Saint, entered Cordoba triumphantly, in siege by his armies since six months back, having been under Moslen power for more than five centuries.

Assisted by bishops, magnates and warriors he purified the Mosque, which was erected a Cathedral under the appellation of Sainte Mary, holding the first liturgical festivities in a chapel dedicated to Saint Clement, founded over the southern wall of the temple. Soon pious foundations and

burials started, and along the Low Middle Ages, there were small changes, the largest being the creation of the Royal Chapel, at the end of the XIII century, to bury kings of Castille, as was done with Ferdinand IV and Alfonso XI. At the end of the XV century the need of an ample cathedral nave was felt, and with the head in what is today the Villaviciosa Chapel, the old Major Chapel was built in the days of the Catholic King, which is isolated today, with a beautiful rosette of the epoch, Gothic caissons among the arcades and many funeral lauds on the floor, many of them moved there recently. Tradition says that Queen Isabella regretted the transforming work.

Half a century later, in 1523, the Corporation of the city agreed to erect another cathedral nave, also inside the Mosque, larger and more sumptuous than the previous one. The Renaissance was in full fledge, and despite the hard opposition of the City Council, who even announced the death penalty for everyone who had a hand in the destruction of the Mosque, a long and loud suit originated, resolved by Emperor Charles I in favor of the ecclesiastic Corporation.

The work of this great cathedral nave lasted practically three centuries, succeeding in it the Gothic, plateresque and Renaissance architectural styles, with projects and labor of very diverse builders, being prominent among them the three generations of the eminent Cordovans Hernán Ruiz. The magnificent Choir, all of it in American mahogany, done by the Sevillian sculptor Duque Cornejo, who is buried there, was completed at the end of the XVIII century. The pulpits already have Verdiguier's French influence, and reached the Napoleonic invasion, which made in Cordoba terrible and reviling depredations.

Christian times brought to the Cathedral of Cordoba unique treasures and works of art, of which something subsists despite the avatars and pillage of own and alien.

In the series of its chapels there is a whole theory of the history of Art, in the grilles, altars, ceramics, retables, paintings and sculptures, jewels and ornaments, and beautiful choir books with a well equipped musical chapel.

With a universal category stands out the Custody of Enrique de Arfe, of the XV century, the best in Spain, twin of the one Toledo, which is the lord of the very diminished richness of the cathedral's treasure.

In paiting stands out the retables made by Pedro de Campaña and de Céspedes, the great Gothic board of the Annunciation, the magnificent Supper and other beautiful retables and paintings of Pablo de Céspedes, and Palomino's paintings, among the red marbles of the great high altar, almost all of it the work of Cordovans.

Sculptures by Pedro de Mena and José de Mora, ivory Christs, the magnificent Saint Paul of Céspedes, revealing the school of Michelangelo ou whose side this Cordovan worked, and other works in marbles and woods give account of the work of gouges and chisels in this Cordovan Cathedral, in which all the modern centuries have left their sediments in the form of magnificent reliques of Spanish Art.

The Mosque-Cathedral of Cordoba was declared a National Monument on the 21st of November of 1882, starting the era of restorations under the direction of conservative architects, of whom the deepest imprint has been that of Mr. Ricardo Velázquez Bosco, who was Director of the High School of Architecture of Madrid.

RAFAEL CASTEJON

49. *The print of the Renaissance is found in this magnificent bronze door-handle on the Ste. Catherine door.*

INDICE

COLECCION IBERICA